THE
TOTALLY
COFFEE
COOKBOOK

The Totally Coffee Cookbook is produced by becker&mayer!, Ltd.
Cover illustration and design: Dick Witt
Interior illustrations: Carolyn Vibbert
Interior design and typesetting: Susan Hernday

Library of Congress Cataloging-in-Publication Data:

Siegel, Helene.
    Totally Coffee Cookbook / by Helene Siegel and Karen Gillingham.
        p. cm.
    ISBN 0-89087-754-8
    1. Cookery (Coffee)   I. Gillingham, Karen.   II. Title.
    TX819.C6S53 1995
    641.6'373—dc20   95-10967
                    CIP

Celestial Arts Publishing
P.O. Box 7123
Berkeley, CA 94707

Other cookbooks in this series:
The Totally Garlic Cookbook
The Totally Chile Pepper Cookbook
The Totally Mushroom Cookbook
The Totally Corn Cookbook
The Totally Cookies Cookbook
The Totally Teatime Cookbook
The Totally Muffins Cookbook

THE
TOTALLY
COFFEE
COOKBOOK

By
Helene Siegel
and
Karen Gillingham

Illustrations by Carolyn Vibbert

CELESTIAL ARTS
BERKELEY, CALIFORNIA

COFFEE HAS ABSOLUTELY NO FOOD VALUE. It may increase cholesterol, aggravate ulcers, trigger irregular heartbeats, and bring on panic attacks and strokes. We know it causes sleeplessness and it is habit forming. And yet we love it.

Its flavor blends superbly with chocolate, vanilla, assorted rich liqueurs like rum and brandy, fruit and nuts, and, of course, milk. It is fantastic in creamy desserts, baked into muffins, cookies and cakes, blended into milkshakes, and stirred into hot toddies.

But most of all we love to drink good quality coffee, steaming hot and freshly brewed. We love it when we wake up in the morning, in the middle of the afternoon, and after a wonderful meal.

It is one of life's great pleasures and it is the one addiction we mean to keep.

The French philosopher Voltaire expressed our sentiments on the caffeine question succinctly, "I have been poisoning myself for more than 80 years," he said, "and I am not yet dead."

INSPIRING
BEVERAGES

HOT MOCHA

A cup of rich, hot mocha is just right when you can't decide between cocoa and coffee.

1 teaspoon chocolate syrup
freshly brewed strong coffee
hot milk
shaved chocolate, cocoa or whipped
cream (optional)

Pour chocolate syrup in large coffee cup or mug. Fill with two thirds coffee and one third milk. Stir and top with shaved chocolate, cocoa, or whipped cream, as desired.

SERVES 1

Iced Coffee
For quick iced coffee, try pouring freshly brewed coffee over coffee-flavored ice cubes.

ARMENIAN COFFEE

Friend and baby sitter, Tamara Tambakian of Los Angeles, taught us this easy method for traditional Armenian or Turkish coffee. It does not call for any special equipment and we understand from Tamara that the future can be read in the sediment left on the bottom of the cup.

1 cup water
2 teaspoons sugar
2 teaspoons finely ground dark roast coffee

In small saucepan, preferably with spout, bring water to boil over medium heat. Add sugar and coffee, stir and return to boil. Remove from heat, stir and return to boil again. Repeat one more time for a total of three stirrings. Pour into espresso cups and serve hot.

SERVES 2

MEXICAN CLAY POT COFFEE

4 cups water
1 small pilóncillo (Mexican brown
   sugar cone) *or* 3 tablespoons dark
   brown sugar
2 cinnamon sticks
½ cup coarsely ground coffee

Combine ingredients in saucepan and bring to a boil. Simmer 5 minutes, return to boil and simmer 5 minutes longer. Strain and serve, preferably from a clay or pottery coffee pot.

SERVES 4

COFFEE SYRUP

Homemade coffee syrup is essential for real coffee ice cream sodas and floats. True addicts should keep a jar on hand in the summer for quick sodas and slush drinks—see page 30. Mix about 3 tablespoons syrup with 1 cup sparkling water or club soda for coffee soda.

1½ cups hot strong coffee
1 cup sugar

Combine coffee and sugar in small saucepan. Bring to boil, reduce to simmer and cook 5 minutes. Let cool, cover, and chill up to 1 week.

MAKES 1½ CUPS

CAPPUCCINO ICE CREAM SODA

¼ cup plus 2 tablespoons coffee syrup
½ cup milk
1 scoop coffee or coffee chocolate
   chip ice cream
½ cup sparkling water

In tall glass, stir together coffee syrup and
milk. Add ice cream scoop and pour in
sparkling water. Serve with straw and spoon.

SERVES 1

ICED MOCHA

This indulgent refresher comes from the former City restaurant in Los Angeles.

> 2 tablespoons chocolate syrup
> 1 cup hot strong coffee
> ¼ cup milk
> 4 ice cubes

Stir together chocolate and coffee. Pour into blender along with milk and ice. Blend at high speed until ice is crushed and drink is frothy. Pour into tall glass and serve.

SERVES 1

THAI ICED COFFEE

You're in for a treat if you've never tasted this rich,
sweet complement to spicy Thai foods.

6 ice cubes
3/4 cup freshly brewed strong coffee
1/4 cup sweetened condensed milk

Blend ice at high speed until shaved.
Transfer to tall glass. Combine coffee and
condensed milk in blender and blend at high
speed until smooth and frothy. Pour over ice
and serve with spoon.

SERVES 1

Breaking the Caffeine Habit
Why anyone would want to stop drinking coffee is
beyond us, but if you do need help, the first chapter
of Caffeine Anonymous has been started in Portland,
Oregon at St. Stephen's Episcopal Church.

MOCHA SHAKE

2 scoops coffee ice cream
1 ½ tablespoons chocolate syrup
½ cup low fat milk

Combine ingredients in blender and blend at high speed until frothy. Serve over ice in tall glass.

SERVES 1

Brewing Tips

Since there are so many options for brewing coffee, not to mention espresso drinks, at home we will not delve into the intricacies of each process here. Far weightier tomes are available for that purpose. However a few simple rules hold true: always use cold water, spring water is best; experiment until you get the proportion of grounds to water correct; and never, ever, reheat coffee. Freshly brewed coffee is best stored in an insulated carafe or thermos.

IRISH COFFEE

When drinking this potent beverage late at night you may want to say a prayer for the whiskey to overpower the caffeine.

1 teaspoon sugar
2 tablespoons Irish whiskey
freshly brewed coffee
whipped cream

Combine sugar and whiskey in a serving cup. Pour in hot coffee and stir. Top with whipped cream to taste. Serve hot with spoon.

SERVES 1

KIOKI COFFEE

2 tablespoons Kahlua or coffee
   liqueur
1 tablespoon brandy
freshly brewed coffee
whipped cream

Combine Kahlua and brandy in a serving glass or mug. Pour in hot coffee, about a cup, and top with whipped cream. Serve hot with spoon.

SERVES 1

CAFÉ BRULOT

1 cinnamon stick, roughly broken
4 whole cloves
peel of ½ orange, slivered
peel of ½ lemon, slivered
4 sugar cubes
¼ cup Cognac
2 tablespoons Grand Marnier or other
    orange liqueur
2 cups hot, strong coffee

In saucepan over low heat, combine cinnamon, cloves, orange and lemon peels, and sugar. Stir in Cognac and liqueur. Using a long match, carefully ignite mixture. Immediately, but slowly, pour in coffee, stirring until flames subside. Pour into small punch cups and serve.

SERVES 4

CAFÉ PARISIAN

2 tablespoons Cognac
1 tablespoon Kahlua or coffee liqueur
1 tablespoon orange liqueur
freshly brewed strong, hot coffee
whipped cream

Combine Cognac and liqueurs in serving cup or glass. Fill with hot coffee. Top with whipped cream and serve.

SERVES 1

WHITE RUSSIAN SHAKE

2 scoops vanilla ice cream
1 tablespoon Kahlua
2 tablespoons vodka

Combine ingredients in blender and blend at high speed until smooth and frothy. Serve over ice in large wine glass.

SERVES 1

How to Store

In an ideal world, we would all purchase fresh beans daily and have no need to worry about storage. However, if you must purchase beans in quantity, we recommend squeezing excess air out of the bag and storing beans in the freezer or in an airtight container at room temperature. Grind as needed.

CAPPUCCINO RUM SHAKE

2 scoops coffee ice cream
2 tablespoons dark rum
⅛ teaspoon cinnamon

Combine ingredients in blender and blend at high speed until smooth and frothy. Pour over ice in large wine glass.

SERVES 1

MUDSLIDE

1 tablespoon Kahlua or coffee liqueur
1 tablespoon Irish cream liqueur
1 tablespoon vodka
2 tablespoons half-and-half or
    heavy cream

Place ingredients over ice in highball glass.
Stir and serve.

SERVES 1

Hidden Health Benefits

Coffee helps asthma sufferers breathe easier, dieters lose weight, and improves hand-eye coordination in the weary. It is reported to increase sexual activity in the elderly. Better think twice before turning to decaf.

TOASTED ALMOND

2 tablespoons Kahlua or
   coffee liqueur
1 tablespoon Amaretto liqueur
half-and-half or milk

Pour Kahlua and Amaretto over ice in high-ball glass. Fill with half-and-half or milk. Stir and serve.

SERVES 1

JAVA FLIP

¾ cup milk
1 egg
2 tablespoons Kahlua or coffee liqueur
1 tablespoon Crème de Cacao
nutmeg

In blender, combine milk, egg, coffee liqueur, and Crème de Cacao. Process until frothy. Pour into tall glass and sprinkle with nutmeg.

SERVES 1

A Coffee Lexicon

ESPRESSO is thick, black coffee, made quickly and to order. A typical serving is 1.5 ounces, served in a tiny cup or demitasse. Any bean can be used to make espresso, as long as it is finely ground and brewed in an espresso maker.

CREMA refers to the thin, light layer of foam that forms on top of a properly brewed espresso. Connoisseurs look for it.

MOCHA refers to the flavor combination of coffee and chocolate—one of the all time greats. The word derives from the Ethiopian city of the same name and a Yemeni coffee that tastes of chocolate.

CAPPUCCINO is a combination of hot espresso and foamed milk served at breakfast in Italy. In the U.S. it is more often a combination of hot espresso and steamed milk, topped with foamed milk, sprinkled with cinnamon or cocoa. The word derives from the brown-hooded monks called Capuchins.

CAFE AU LAIT is a drink of hot coffee served with hot or steamed milk, often served in wide porcelain bowls at breakfast in France.

CAFE LATTE, the Italian version of coffee and milk, is a combination of espresso with lots of steamed milk, topped with a short crown of foam.

MACCHIATO is a shot of espresso topped with a dab of foamed milk and served in a small cup.

Ice Creams
Puddings
Toppings
&
Treats

ESPRESSO ICE

You don't need an ice cream maker or any other special equipment to make this refreshing iced dessert.

½ cup sugar
1 cup water
1 cup freshly brewed espresso, French or Italian roast
whipped cream (optional)

Combine sugar and water in small saucepan. Bring to boil, stirring frequently, until sugar is dissolved and liquid is clear. Remove from heat. Stir in coffee, pour into 8-inch metal cake pan and cool to room temperature. Freeze until solid, about 4 hours.

Before serving, remove from freezer and let sit a few minutes to soften. Break into large pieces with blunt knife and transfer to food processor. Pulse until slush is formed. Serve in chilled wine glasses and top with dollop of whipped cream, if desired.

SERVES 4

Bean Basics

There are two types of beans in the world: arabica and robusta. Arabicas, grown at higher altitudes, are better quality and used for higher priced specialty coffees. Robustas—primarily used for the canned blends and instant coffees typically found in supermarkets—are grown at lower altitudes on heartier plants and are therefore less costly. Unfortunately they don't taste as good and contain twice the caffeine of arabicas, so beware the cheap cup of coffee. You may pay for it in the middle of the night.

CAPPUCCINO BLIZZARD

An adult version of those sticky, sweet, cool slushes that kids eat in the summer. Coffee syrup is a lifesaver in the summer refrigerator of the seriously caffeine addicted.

¼ cup coffee syrup, (page 11)
1 tablespoon cream or milk
8 ice cubes, crushed or shaved

In small bowl, stir together coffee syrup and cream or milk. Place crushed ice in chilled wine glass. Pour coffee mixture over, stir once or twice and serve.

SERVES 1

WHIPPED COFFEE CREAM

1 cup heavy cream
2 teaspoons instant espresso powder
3 tablespoons confectioners' sugar

In deep bowl, combine cream and instant espresso. Refrigerate 10 minutes. Starting at low speed of electric mixer, beat cream, gradually increasing speed to high and slowly adding confectioners' sugar, until cream is thick enough to hold shape. Serve as topping for desserts or hot or cold drinks.

MAKES 2 CUPS

COFFEE PISTACHIO
ICE CREAM CAKE

For those who have never lost their taste for ice cream cake, this great make-ahead summer dessert keeps about a week in the freezer.

30 thin chocolate wafers
4 tablespoons butter, melted
1½ pints coffee ice cream, softened
½ cup coarsely ground raw pistachios
2 ounces semisweet chocolate, chopped

Finely grind chocolate wafers in food processor. Combine in bowl with butter and mix with fingertips until evenly moistened. Press into bottom and sides of lightly oiled 9-inch glass pie plate or tart pan with removable bottom. Freeze ½ hour.

Remove crust from freezer and fill with softened ice cream. With spatula, smooth from middle to outside edges to evenly fill pie. Freeze ½ hour.

Remove from freezer. Sprinkle nuts in 1-inch circle around top to form edge and lightly press. Melt chocolate in bowl over simmering water. Dip tines of fork in chocolate and drizzle over ice cream and nuts to decorate. Freeze ½ hour, cover with aluminum foil and freeze at least 4 hours to set. Cut in wedges with sharp knife dipped in hot water to serve.

SERVES 6

COFFEE COCONUT PARFAIT

*For the truly serious dieter who must have coffee—
a low calorie yogurt parfait.*

½ cup grated unsweetened coconut
½ cup sliced almonds
3 (8-ounce) containers coffee yogurt
8 teaspoons Amaretto liqueur

Place coconut and almonds on separate
baking sheets and toast in an oven set at
350 degrees F—5 minutes for coconut and 10
minutes for almonds.

Fill four wine glasses one-third full with
coffee yogurt. Sprinkle each with 1 tablespoon
coconut, 1 tablespoon almonds and 1 teaspoon
Amaretto. Repeat layers and serve or cover
with plastic and chill until serving time.

SERVES 4

Decaf Dilemma

One out of four cups of coffee drunk in America is decaffeinated. Usually caffeine is washed away using the direct contact, or methyl chloride process, which consists of removing caffeine with a chemical solvent which is burned off during roasting. The other method, which is more expensive and less popular, is Swiss water. With this method the beans are soaked in several hot water baths and charcoal filters remove the caffeine. Even quality roasters prefer the chemical process since the coffee retains much better flavor, although research is ongoing to improve the water process. In the meantime don't lose sleep over the chemicals since virtually none can be detected in a brewed cup. In 1989 the FDA declared that the risk of cancer for a heavy lifetime user was one in a million.

CHOCOLATE ESPRESSO MOUSSE

Deep, dark chocolate with an edge of espresso in a smooth-as-silk French mousse. What could be better?

6 ounces semisweet chocolate, chopped
2 tablespoons butter
2 tablespoons sugar
4 eggs, separated
3 tablespoons brewed espresso, cold
¼ teaspoon salt

Combine chocolate, butter, and sugar in heavy saucepan over low heat. Cook, stirring frequently, until smooth and melted. Let cool 10 minutes.

In mixing bowl, beat egg yolks until pale and smooth. Gradually add chocolate mixture and beat well to combine. Mix in coffee and salt.

In another clean bowl, whisk egg whites until stiff, glossy peaks form. Gently fold into chocolate mixture in 3 parts until white just disappears. Spoon into 6 small dessert cups or glass bowl and chill 4 hours. Serve cold with Chocolate-Dipped Espresso Beans (page 54).

SERVES 6

WHITE CHOCOLATE AU LAIT SOUFFLÉS

Because these soufflés have no stiffly beaten egg whites, they can be prepared ahead of time and refrigerated until ready to bake. If chilled, add 5 minutes to baking time. For lighter soufflés, fold in 2 stiffly beaten egg whites just before pouring into dishes and bake immediately.

butter, room temperature
sugar
2 tablespoons instant espresso powder
⅓ cup milk
6 ounces white chocolate, chopped
5 eggs
½ cup heavy cream
1 (8-ounce) package cream cheese,
    softened and cubed
cocoa and confectioners' sugar for dusting

Preheat oven to 350 degrees F. Butter 6 (6-ounce) individual soufflé or custard cups. Sprinkle with sugar, shaking out excess.

In small saucepan, combine espresso, milk, and chocolate. Place over low heat, stirring frequently, until chocolate melts. Remove from heat and cool slightly.

Place eggs in bowl of food processor or blender. Add cream and process to mix. With machine running, slowly pour cooled chocolate mixture through top. Add cream cheese, a few cubes at a time, and process until smooth. Pour into prepared dishes and bake in center of oven about 20 minutes or until edges are set but centers jiggle slightly when oven rack is gently shaken. Remove from oven, sift cocoa and powdered sugar over tops, and serve.

SERVES 6

MOCHA STUFFED PEACHES

This cozy dessert is like a fruit crumble enhanced with the delectable flavors of coffee and cocoa.

6 large freestone peaches, peeled, halved, and pitted
1½ cups macaroon cookie crumbs
½ cup sugar
¼ cup Dutch process cocoa
1 teaspoon instant espresso powder
2 egg yolks
¼ cup Kahlua or coffee liqueur

Preheat oven to 375 degrees F. Grease a shallow baking dish just big enough to fit peaches snugly. Scoop out scant 1 tablespoon peach pulp from each peach half and reserve.

Arrange peach halves, cut-side-up, in prepared dish.

In food processor, combine peach pulp, cookie crumbs, sugar, cocoa, espresso powder, yolks, and liqueur. Process to make paste. Divide mixture evenly among peach halves—don't be concerned about spilling over peaches. Bake about 20 minutes. Serve warm or at room temperature.

SERVES 6

Commercial Blends

Most of the coffee we drink is a blend of seven or eight types of beans. There are three general types: Brazilian, created for low price and mass distribution; Mild, made of higher quality arabica beans, blended for flavor and balance and not necessarily mild tasting; and Robusta, a combination of lower priced robustas with some higher quality African beans.

CRÈME BRÛLÉE CAFÉ

3 cups heavy cream
⅓ cup sugar
½ teaspoon vanilla
2 teaspoons instant
   espresso powder
6 egg yolks, lightly beaten
1 cup light brown sugar

In top of double boiler or bowl over simmering water, combine cream, sugar, vanilla, and espresso powder. Stir in yolks. Cook, stirring frequently, until mixture coats back of spoon, about 8 minutes. Pour into shallow 1½-quart casserole. Stir to cool slightly. Place plastic wrap directly on surface and refrigerate 1 to 2 hours.

Preheat broiler. Sift brown sugar evenly over top and set casserole in shallow bed of

crushed ice in baking pan. Broil about 6 inches
from heat until sugar melts and bubbles,
watching carefully to prevent burning.

Remove from pan and chill about 10 minutes. Serve some caramelized topping with
each portion.

SERVES 6

The Coffee Tree

*The original coffee tree, a perennial evergreen
bush, genus* Coffea, *is from the area now known as
Ethiopia in Africa. The tree does not bear fruit until
its sixth year, when it begins to bear the white jas-
mine-scented blossoms that become cherries or beans.
It continues to produce for 15 years. Since they ripen
at different rates, each red cherry must be hand-
picked and then processed to remove the parchment
envelope inside, which contains two beans, ready for
cleaning, sorting, and roasting.*

COFFEE INDIAN PUDDING

Indian Pudding is a classic New England dessert made of cornmeal and molasses. What it lacks in sophistication, it more than makes up for in taste.

4 cups milk
4 teaspoons instant espresso powder
½ cup yellow cornmeal
½ cup dark brown sugar
¼ cup sugar
¼ cup molasses
½ teaspoon salt
½ stick butter
½ teaspoon ground ginger
½ teaspoon cinnamon
coffee ice cream

Preheat oven to 300 degrees F. Grease 1½-quart casserole. In small bowl, combine 1 cup milk and 1 teaspoon espresso powder. Set aside.

In top of double boiler, heat remaining milk and espresso powder. Gradually stir in cornmeal. Set over simmering water and cook and stir 10 to 15 minutes, or until creamy. Stir in sugars, molasses, salt, butter, ginger and cinnamon. Transfer to prepared casserole and pour reserved milk mixture over top. Set casserole in pan of hot water and bake 2½ to 3 hours, until set. Serve warm with coffee ice cream or Whipped Coffee Cream (see page 31).

SERVES 8

CAPPUCCINO BREAD PUDDING

What a great Sunday breakfast for the truly indulgent.

> 6 eggs
> ³/₄ cup sugar
> 3 cups half-and-half
> ¼ cup Kahlua or coffee liqueur
> ¼ cup brewed espresso, room temperature
> 1 teaspoon vanilla
> 6 cups (1-inch) cubes dry French bread,
>   crusts removed
> 1 tablespoon sugar plus ½ teaspoon
>   cinnamon, for sprinkling

In large mixing bowl, whisk together eggs and sugar. Add half-and-half, Kahlua, espresso, and vanilla and whisk. Add bread, mix to evenly moisten and let sit 1 hour.

Preheat oven to 325 degrees F.

Pour mixture into buttered glass loaf pan or ceramic soufflé dish. Place in larger roasting pan filled with 2 inches water and bake 1 hour.

Carefully remove from oven, and sprinkle top with cinnamon sugar. Return to oven and bake 25 to 30 minutes longer, until center feels firm when pressed and top is crusty. Serve hot or cold.

SERVES 8

Coffee as a Commodity

Coffee is second only to oil in world trade. Sixty nations—mostly third world and situated along the coffee belt, located twenty-five degrees north and south of the equator—depend on it for their economies. Brazil is the number one producer, and the United States the number one consumer of coffee.

TIRAMISU

This whipped espresso and alcohol-drenched dessert is an international favorite.

> 6 egg yolks
> 1 cup sugar
> 1½ cups mascarpone cheese
> 3 egg whites
> ½ cup cold espresso
> ¼ cup rum
> 1 (3-ounce) package ladyfingers
> cocoa for dusting

With electric mixer, beat egg yolks and sugar together until light and creamy. Add mascarpone, 2 tablespoons at a time, beating continuously at medium speed until thick and creamy.

In another bowl, whisk egg whites until stiff peaks form. Gently fold into cheese mixture in three batches.

Combine espresso and rum in small bowl. Pull apart ladyfingers and arrange on bottom of 9-inch square baking pan. Drizzle cookies with half the espresso mixture to evenly soak. Spread layer of half cheese mixture on top and repeat with cookies, espresso and cheese. Dust with cocoa, cover and chill at least 3 hours. Cut into squares and lift with spatula to serve.

SERVES 6

DEMITASSE TRUFFLES

8 ounces semisweet chocolate, chopped
²/₃ cup heavy cream
2 teaspoons instant espresso powder
¼ stick butter
3 tablespoons Dutch process cocoa
¼ teaspoon cinnamon (optional)
confectioners' sugar

Line 8 x 4-inch loaf pan with plastic wrap.

In top of double boiler or bowl, melt chocolate over simmering water, stirring until smooth. Set aside.

In small saucepan, combine cream and espresso powder. Stir over medium heat just until espresso is dissolved. Gradually stir cream into melted chocolate until smooth. Stir in butter, cocoa, and cinnamon, if using. Blend thoroughly. Transfer mixture to prepared pan and spread to make even layer. Cover and refrigerate until firm.

Remove chocolate from pan and peel away plastic wrap. With sharp thin knife, cut into ¾-inch cubes. Arrange in single layer on plastic-lined baking sheet. Cover and refrigerate or freeze until ready to serve.

Place powdered sugar in plastic bag. Add chocolate cubes, a few at a time, and gently shake to coat with sugar.

MAKES ABOUT 36

FROZEN CAPPUCCINO CUPS

3 eggs, separated, room temperature
1 tablespoon sugar
2 tablespoons cold strong coffee
¼ cup Kahlua or coffee liqueur
½ cup heavy cream

Line muffin pan with foil cups.

In top of double boiler, using wire whisk, beat egg yolks and sugar until light and fluffy. Gradually add coffee and liqueur, beating constantly. Place over simmering water and continue to beat just until mixture is foamy and thick, about 5 minutes. Transfer to large bowl and place inside larger bowl filled with ice water. Continue to beat until cool.

In separate bowl, beat egg whites until stiff but not dry. In another bowl, beat cream until very thick. Carefully fold egg whites and whipped cream into coffee mixture. Spoon into prepared muffin pans and freeze.

Transfer to refrigerator about 30 minutes or let stand at room temperature 10 minutes before serving. Garnish each cup with Chocolate-Dipped Espresso Beans (page 54).

MAKES 8

CHOCOLATE-DIPPED ESPRESSO BEANS

Here is a tip from Karen's food styling bag of tricks: If chocolate becomes too cool, re-warm to dipping consistency with a hair dryer.

4 ounces semisweet chocolate,
  coarsely chopped
1 tablespoon grated semisweet chocolate
1 cup dark roasted coffee beans

Place chocolate in small dry bowl set over simmering water. Stir until smooth. Chocolate should not exceed 115 degrees F on candy thermometer. Remove bowl from water and slowly stir in grated chocolate, stirring until melted. Cool to 90 degrees F.

Using tweezers or two fingers, dip each coffee bean into chocolate. Lift from bowl and shake gently to remove excess chocolate. Place on waxed paper-lined baking sheet. Store in covered container with waxed paper between layers.

MAKES 1 CUP

The Roast's the Thing

Raw, unroasted beans are green or yellow and have no coffee flavor. It is the roasting process that cooks them and develops their aroma and flavor. Each type has an ideal roasting time, but the average is about ten minutes at 390 degrees F. After roasting, beans must be quickly and carefully cooled and stored, since flavor and quality start to deteriorate immediately.

ESPRESSO HOT FUDGE SAUCE

This rich, dark sauce is perfect on a scoop of good vanilla ice cream, sprinkled with chunks of salted almonds.

⅓ cup freshly brewed strong coffee
⅓ cup brown sugar
½ cup Dutch process cocoa
pinch salt
2 tablespoons butter, in small pieces
3 tablespoons heavy cream
1 teaspoon instant espresso powder

Combine coffee and brown sugar in small heavy saucepan over medium heat. Cook, stirring frequently, until sugar is melted. Add cocoa and salt and whisk until smooth.

Reduce heat to low. Whisk in butter and cream, and then whisk in instant espresso. Stir until dissolved. Serve immediately over ice cream.

This sauce may be stored for up to two weeks in the refrigerator. Reheat in a heavy saucepan over low heat, stirring frequently.

MAKES ¾ CUPS

It's a Grind

Small electric grinders make fresh, whole-bean coffee easy to make at home. It is worth experimenting to find the right size ground for your coffee maker. In general, the faster the brewing method, the finer the grind. Espresso should be ground the finest, drip should be medium ground, plunger medium-fine, and percolator coarse.

COOKIES
&
CAKES

MOCHA WAFERS

We first tasted these thin, crumbly wafers at
The Bakery in Los Angeles. They set the standard
for decadent mocha treats.

4 ounces unsweetened chocolate, chopped
2½ cups semisweet chocolate chips
1 stick butter
4 eggs
½ cup all-purpose flour
½ teaspoon baking powder
½ teaspoon salt
1½ cups sugar
1 tablespoon finely ground espresso beans
2 teaspoons vanilla

Combine unsweetened chocolate, 1½ cups
chocolate chips, and butter in medium heavy

saucepan. Melt over low heat, stirring frequently, until smooth. Set aside.

In small bowl, combine flour, baking powder, and salt.

In another bowl, with electric mixer, beat eggs and sugar until thick and pale. Beat in ground coffee and vanilla. Gently stir in chocolate mixture, then stir in flour and remaining cup of chips. Let sit 15 minutes.

Preheat oven to 350 degrees F. Line cookie sheets with parchment paper.

Drop by generous tablespoonfuls, 2 inches apart, on prepared sheet. Bake about 10 minutes, until puffed and shiny and tops are cracked. Let cool on sheet 5 minutes, then carefully transfer to racks to cool.

MAKES 32

COFFEE ALMOND BISCOTTI

These subtly flavored dunking cookies make an excellent afternoon snack.

1 stick butter, softened
¾ cup sugar
2 eggs
½ teaspoon almond extract
1 tablespoon instant espresso powder
2½ cups all-purpose flour
½ cup finely ground almonds
2 teaspoons baking powder
¼ teaspoon salt
4 ounces semisweet chocolate, chopped
  (optional)

Preheat oven to 350 degrees F.

Beat together butter and sugar until light and fluffy. Add eggs, almond extract, and espresso. Beat well.

In another bowl, combine flour, almonds, baking powder, and salt. Add to butter mixture and lightly beat until dough forms.

Transfer to floured board and lightly knead. Divide in half and press each into 8 x 4-inch loaf. Transfer to uncoated baking sheet and bake 40 to 45 minutes, until firm.

Remove from oven, leaving oven on. Cool on sheet 10 minutes. Then transfer to cutting board and cut across width into ½-inch thick slices. Place on sheet, cut-side-up, and bake 10 minutes longer on each side. Let cool and store or coat with chocolate.

To coat: melt chocolate in small saucepan over pan of simmering water. Spread about ½ teaspoon chocolate over half of one side of each cookie. Place on plate and chill until chocolate sets. Store at room temperature.

MAKES 24 LARGE BISCOTTI

ZEBRA ESPRESSO BARS

2 (3-ounce) packages cream cheese,
    softened
3 eggs
1 tablespoon instant espresso powder
1 ½ cups sugar
1 cup flour
¾ stick butter, cut in small pieces
½ cup Dutch process cocoa
¼ teaspoon baking powder
¼ teaspoon salt
½ cup strong hot espresso

Preheat oven to 325 degrees F. Grease and
flour 9-inch square baking pan.

In bowl, combine cream cheese, 1 egg,
espresso powder, ¼ cup sugar, and 2 tablespoons
each flour and butter. Beat until light and fluffy.
Set aside.

In separate bowl, sift remaining sugar and flour with cocoa, baking powder, and salt. Stir remaining butter into hot coffee. Add to dry ingredients and stir to blend. Beat in remaining eggs, one at a time, beating well after each addition.

Spread mixture evenly in prepared pan. Spoon cheese mixture, in several separate pools, over chocolate batter, spacing evenly. Run knife through batters to marbleize. Bake about 30 minutes. Cool on wire rack, then cut into 3 x 1½-inch bars. Store in refrigerator.

MAKES 18

COFFEE KISSES

1 teaspoon instant espresso powder
1¼ cups sugar
½ cup water
3 egg whites
¼ teaspoon cream of tartar
dash salt

Preheat oven to 200 degrees F. Line large baking sheet with foil, shiny-side-down.

In 2-quart saucepan, combine instant espresso, 1 cup sugar, and water. Stir over low heat until coffee and sugar dissolve. Bring to boil over medium heat. Boil until candy thermometer registers 240 degrees F, about 15 minutes, brushing down sides of pan often with pastry brush dipped in water. Mixture will be very thick. Remove from heat.

In bowl of mixer, beat egg whites with cream of tartar and salt on high speed until soft peaks form. Add remaining sugar and beat until stiff peaks form. Beat in hot coffee syrup in 2 to 3 batches. Continue to beat on high speed 4 to 5 minutes, until meringue is very thick. Using pastry bag fitted with large star tip, pipe meringue into 1½-inch kisses onto prepared baking sheet.

Bake on center rack of oven 4 hours. Without opening door, turn heat off and let kisses dry in oven 2 hours longer or until crisp. Store in airtight container.

MAKES ABOUT 30

ESPRESSO HAZELNUT CHIP COOKIES

A grown-up version of the chocolate chip cookie—
always a wonderful way to help milk go down.

1 ¼ cups all-purpose flour
½ teaspoon baking soda
¼ teaspoon salt
1 stick butter, softened
1 cup brown sugar
1 egg
1 teaspoon vanilla
2 tablespoons instant espresso
½ cup semisweet chocolate chips
½ cup roughly chopped hazelnuts

Preheat oven to 350 degrees F. Lightly grease cookie sheets.

Combine flour, baking soda, and salt.

    In another bowl, beat together butter
and sugar until smooth. Beat in egg and
vanilla. Beat in espresso. Add flour mixture
and gently beat until flour disappears. Stir in
chips and hazelnuts.

    Drop by tablespoonfuls on prepared sheet
and bake 12 to 14 minutes, until edges are
golden. Transfer to racks to cool.

MAKES 26

QUICK CAPPUCCINO COFFEE CAKE

Not too sweet or chocolatey, this easy, one-pan cake is a good choice for a company brunch.

10 ounces milk chocolate
1 ½ tablespoons instant espresso
1 stick butter, softened
½ cup sugar
4 eggs
1 tablespoon vanilla
½ teaspoon cinnamon
½ teaspoon salt
1 cup all-purpose flour

GLAZE
¼ cup confectioners' sugar
2 tablespoons Kahlua

Preheat oven to 350 degrees F. Grease 8-inch square cake pan and line with parchment.

Melt chocolate and coffee in heavy pan over low heat, stirring frequently.

With electric mixer, beat butter until light and fluffy. Gradually beat in sugar. Add eggs and vanilla and beat well. Beat in melted chocolate mixture, cinnamon, and salt. Add flour and beat until batter is smooth and thick. Pour into pan and bake ½ hour, until tester comes out clean. Set aside to cool.

Make glaze by whisking together sugar and Kahlua until smooth. Brush over cake. Cut in squares to serve.

MAKES 20 SQUARES

CAPPUCCINO CHIP MUFFINS

These are great for stuffing in your purse or backpack when you need a caffeine fix to go.

2 tablespoons instant espresso
1 tablespoon hot water
2 eggs
½ cup brown sugar
½ cup heavy cream
2 tablespoons low fat milk
½ stick butter, melted
1 ½ cups all-purpose flour
¼ cup whole wheat flour
2 ½ teaspoons baking powder
¼ teaspoon salt
⅓ cup mini chocolate chips

Preheat oven to 375 degrees F. Grease muffin tins or line with paper cups.

Stir together espresso and water until dissolved. Set aside.

In large mixing bowl, whisk together eggs and sugar until smooth. Add cream, milk, butter, and espresso. Whisk to combine.

In another bowl, combine flours, baking powder, and salt. Stir with fork. Add dry ingredients to liquid and stir by hand until flour disappears. Stir in chocolate chips.

Fill muffin cups nearly to top. Bake about 20 minutes, or until tester comes out clean.

MAKES 12

MOCHA CHEESECAKE TART

For unrequited fans of cheesecake and coffee, here is an all-in-one cake with a dollop of milk chocolate so no one feels deprived.

1 cup graham cracker crumbs
½ cup ground blanched almonds
5 tablespoons butter, softened
3 eggs
½ cup sugar
3 (8-ounce) packages cream cheese, softened
1 teaspoon vanilla
3 ounces milk chocolate, melted
2 tablespoons instant espresso
1 tablespoon Kahlua or coffee liqueur

Preheat oven to 350 degrees F.

Combine crumbs, almonds, and butter with pastry blender and press into bottom of 9-inch springform pan.

In electric mixer, blend eggs and sugar until smooth. Beat in cream cheese, a bit at a time, until smooth. Beat in remaining ingredients. Pour over crust and bake 1 hour. Turn oven off and let sit in oven 1 hour longer. Chill and remove sides before serving.

SERVES 8

MOCHA STREUSEL COFFEE CAKE

¼ cup light brown sugar
2 ounces milk chocolate, chopped
1 tablespoon butter, cut in small pieces
2 teaspoons instant espresso
2 teaspoons cinnamon
1¼ cups plus 1 tablespoon
    all-purpose flour
½ cup sugar
2 teaspoons baking powder
½ teaspoon salt
½ cup milk
1 egg
3 tablespoons butter, melted

Preheat oven to 375 degrees F. Grease
8-inch square baking pan.

For streusel, gently combine sugar, chocolate, butter, espresso, cinnamon, and 1 tablespoon flour. Set aside.

In separate bowl, combine remaining flour, sugar, baking powder, and salt.

In another bowl, beat milk with egg and melted butter to blend. Pour all at once into dry mixture and stir just until evenly moistened. Pour into prepared pan. Sprinkle streusel evenly over top. Bake about 20 minutes or until toothpick inserted in center comes out clean. Cool slightly, then cut into squares.

SERVES 9

CAPPUCCINO CREAM PUFFS

1 cup water
¾ stick butter
⅓ cup plus 1 teaspoon sugar
dash salt
1⅓ cups sifted flour
6 eggs, room temperature
1 egg yolk
1 cup milk
6 tablespoons Kahlua or coffee liqueur
1 tablespoon each confectioners' sugar and cocoa
1 teaspoon instant espresso powder

Preheat oven to 425 degrees F. Grease baking sheets.

In small saucepan, combine water with

butter, 1 teaspoon sugar, and salt. Bring to boil. Remove from heat and add 1 cup flour all at once. Stir rapidly with wooden spoon until thoroughly mixed. Return pan to medium heat and continue beating until dough leaves sides of pan and forms ball. Remove pan from heat and add four eggs, one at a time, beating well after each.

Using pastry bag fitted with ½-inch plain tip or plastic bag with corner snipped to leave ½-inch opening, pipe 1-inch mounds of dough onto prepared baking sheets.

In small bowl, beat 1 egg with 1 teaspoon water. Brush mixture over dough mounds. Bake 20 minutes or until mounds are golden and doubled in size. With sharp knife, make slit in side of each puff to allow steam to escape. Return puffs to turned-off oven with door ajar and leave for 10 minutes, until insides are dry.

Cool on wire rack. Meanwhile, in bowl, using wooden spoon, beat remaining ⅓ cup sugar, ⅓ cup flour, one egg, and egg yolk until smooth.

In small saucepan, heat milk to simmering. Gradually pour into flour mixture then return to pan and cook over medium heat, stirring constantly, until very thick, about 3 minutes. Stir in coffee liqueur. Pour into bowl, cover and chill.

Split puffs in half. Mound about 2 teaspoons cream mixture onto each bottom. Replace top halves.

Combine powdered sugar, cocoa, and espresso powder and sift over cream puffs. Chill until serving time.

MAKES 36 PUFFS, 12 SERVINGS

A Cup of Joe

Since the Boston Tea Party, coffee has ruled the American breakfast table. The current popularity of specialty coffees is actually a return to the original concept. Canned, ready-ground coffee was only introduced in the 19th century. Prior to that most coffee was arabica, and ground either at home or by the merchant. It gradually became a thin, bitter brew with the introduction of cheaper robusta beans and mass distribution. American coffee reached its low point in the late 1950s, with the marriage of canned robusta blends and the electric percolator.

The tide started to turn in the early 60s when two pioneers of gourmet food marketing, Zabar's of New York and Peet's of San Francisco, started selling whole beans. Now, thirty years later, fresh espresso is available at nearly every shopping mall in the land. Who said the world isn't a better place?

MARBLED MOCHA TART

1 stick butter, softened
¾ cup sugar
1 teaspoon vanilla
½ cup sifted Dutch process cocoa
1 cup flour
6 ounces white chocolate, chopped
6 ounces semisweet chocolate, chopped
1 cup heavy cream
1 tablespoon instant espresso powder

Preheat oven to 375 degrees F.

In food processor, combine butter, sugar, and vanilla and process until smooth. Add cocoa powder and process to blend. Add flour and pulse until mixture begins to hold together. Press mixture onto bottom and sides

of 10-inch tart pan with removable bottom.
Pierce bottom all over with fork.

Place in freezer 10 minutes. Bake 15 minutes. Set aside to cool.

Place the two chocolates in separate bowls. In saucepan bring cream to gentle boil. Stir in espresso powder. Pour ½ cup hot espresso cream into each bowl. Stir until smooth. Fill tart shell with dark filling. Pour five separate pools of white chocolate filling over dark chocolate filling. Pull tip of knife through fillings to marbleize. Chill until set.

SERVES 12

Secret
Ingredients

CHICKEN CHILI
A LA JAVA

¼ cup vegetable oil
3 pounds chicken thighs and/or legs
1 large onion, chopped
4 garlic cloves, chopped
2 tablespoons flour
1 (14-ounce) can tomatoes, drained
  and chopped
1 (13-ounce) can tomatillos, drained
  and chopped
1 (14½-ounce) can chicken broth
1 tablespoon instant coffee powder
2 (7-ounce) cans diced mild green chiles
1 jalapeño chile, stemmed, seeded,
  and diced
2 teaspoons dried crumbled oregano
1 teaspoon ground coriander

1 teaspoon ground cumin
salt and pepper
garnishes: lime wedges, chopped red onion, cilantro leaves, cubed avocado, shredded Jack cheese, and sour cream

Heat oil in large skillet over high heat. Fry chicken pieces, turning frequently, until evenly browned, about 15 minutes. Transfer chicken to large oven-proof casserole and set aside.

Pour off all but 2 tablespoons oil from skillet. Add onion and garlic and cook over medium heat until soft. Add flour and cook, stirring frequently, 3 minutes longer. Stir in tomatoes, tomatillos, broth, coffee powder, green chiles, jalapeño, oregano, coriander, and cumin. Bring to boil. Pour over chicken in casserole. Cover with foil and bake 45 minutes. Remove from oven, loosen foil and set aside to cool.

When chicken is cool enough to handle, remove skin and bones. Cut meat into bite-sized pieces and place in large pan with sauce from casserole. Place over medium heat until heated through. Season to taste with salt and pepper. Serve in bowls with limes, onion, cilantro, avocado, cheese, and sour cream, if desired.

SERVES 8

Key Players in Coffee History

• *Kaldi of Kaffa, a goatherd, was the first to brew and drink coffee, according to Arabian legend. He was inspired by his high-spirited goats, who seemed more energetic after munching on fallen coffee berries.*

• *The Grand Vizir of the Ottoman empire prohibited coffee and closed the coffee houses of Turkey in 1656. The penalty for drinking coffee was nothing too serious—just a dunk in the Bosphorus in a leather satchel.*

• *Francesco Procopio de Coltelli of Sicily is credited with starting the first cafe in Paris, Le Procope, in*

1686—an establishment that is still in business. It has been the hangout of such luminaries as Voltaire, Diderot, and Robespierre.

- *Louis XIV of France was given a gift of a coffee plant by the Mayor of Amsterdam in 1714. When a young French naval officer chose a plant from the king's garden to bring along on a visit to Martinique in the Caribbean, he started what was to become the world's largest coffee crop.*

- *King Gustav III of Sweden researched the health benefits of coffee vs. tea in his own quirky way back in the 18th century. He commuted the death sentence of twin convicts, instead sentencing them to life so that doctors could study their differences: One drank only coffee, the other tea. Since the tea drinker died first, at the age of 83, Sweden became a country of coffee drinkers.*

- *President Theodore Roosevelt, the man who gave us the "teddy" bear, also promoted the house blend at the Maxwell House Hotel in Nashville, Tennessee, thereby creating the catchy slogan, "good to the last drop."*

CUP O' JOE BARBECUE SAUCE

1 cup strong coffee
1 cup catsup
¼ cup cider vinegar
¼ light brown sugar
¼ cup finely chopped onion
1 tablespoon Worcestershire sauce
1 tablespoon Dijon mustard
¼ teaspoon dried crushed thyme
salt and pepper

Combine ingredients in saucepan. Bring to boil, reduce to simmer and cook 20 minutes. Season to taste with salt and pepper.

MAKES ABOUT 2 CUPS

HAM WITH RED-EYE GRAVY

1 teaspoon oil
1 (¼-inch thick) ham slice
¾ cup strong coffee
2 cups hot cooked grits

Heat oil in large skillet. Add ham slice and fry, turning often, until well browned on both sides. Transfer to heated platter and keep warm. Add coffee to skillet and cook and stir, scraping up browned bits, until gravy turns reddish-brown, about 5 minutes. Serve ham with grits and pass the gravy!

SERVES 2 TO 3

CAFFEINE BEANS

1 pound dried small white beans
2 cups coffee
3 cups water
½ pound bacon, cooked and crumbled
¾ cup light brown sugar
¾ cup catsup
1 tablespoon dry mustard
salt, pepper, and liquid hickory seasoning

Place beans in large saucepan. Add coffee and water and bring to boil. Boil 2 minutes and remove from heat. Cover and set aside 1 hour.

Return beans to boil. Reduce heat and simmer, covered, 1 hour. Skim off any foam. Stir in bacon, brown sugar, catsup and mustard.

Preheat oven to 275 degrees F.

Transfer beans to oven-proof casserole with lid. Cover and bake 2 to 3 hours, stirring occasionally, and adding more water or coffee if dry. Season to taste with salt, pepper, and hickory seasoning.

SERVES 8

Varietals

With varietals, or specialty coffees, the beans derive from similar soil, and so should have a distinctive flavor reflecting that geography. When the world was a simpler place, we only had names like Jamaica Blue Mountain or Kona to keep track of. Now there are many more varietals to know, like Sulawesi and Ethiopia Sidamo.

In general, African and Arabian beans have rich flavor, full body, and medium acidity. Coffees from Indonesia and the Pacific are known for their low acidity, full body, and acidic flavors. American beans are considered light-bodied with a clean, lively taste.

CHIPOTLE CAFE MOLE

This thick, rich salsa is like a simplified mole.

4 large tomatoes
3 garlic cloves, unpeeled
1 onion, unpeeled and halved
8 to 10 dried chipotle chiles, stemmed
1 (14½-ounce can) chicken stock
1 quart water
⅓ cup sesame seeds
½ cup slivered almonds
¼ teaspoon cinnamon
2 teaspoons salt
¼ cup whole coffee beans

Preheat broiler. Arrange tomatoes, garlic, and onion on tray and broil, turning frequently, until evenly charred. Let cool slightly, remove garlic and onion skins and transfer to food processor. Process until roughly puréed.

Transfer mixture to large pot and add chipotles, chicken stock, and water. Bring to boil, reduce to simmer and cook, uncovered, 20 minutes.

Meanwhile, toast sesame seeds in small, dry skillet over medium-low heat until aromatic and golden. Toast almonds in pan and add to food processor.

Transfer hot chipotle mixture to food processor and purée. Pour back into pot, stir in ground sesame seeds, almonds, cinnamon, salt, and coffee beans. Bring to boil, reduce to a simmer, and cook 30 to 40 minutes to thicken to taste. Remove and discard coffee beans with slotted spoon or pass through sieve for finer texture. Serve hot with grilled chicken, pork, or beef.

MAKES 2 QUARTS

Arabic Coffee Cultures

When the coffee plant was brought across the Red Sea to Yemen from Ethiopia, it spread deep roots into Arab soil. Since alcohol is forbidden, coffee, or "qah-wah" was recognized for its powerful stimulating qualities by the most devout Muslims, the dervishes, who prayed and whirled until they collapsed.

In contemporary Middle Eastern homes, ritual still surrounds the serving and drinking of coffee. It must be offered to everyone who enters the house. It must be served swiftly and according to each drinker's taste. To refuse coffee is an insult to the host and even children are taught to brew the thick, sweet beverage.